Your Word

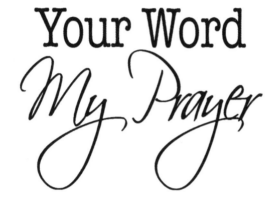
My Prayer

Spiritual nourishment from Scripture and prayers that empower

Paul Bunday

D1405378

First published in 2007
Copyright ©
All rights reserved. No part of this publication
may be reproduced in any form without prior
permission from the publisher.
British Library Cataloguing in Publication Data.
A catalogue record for this book is available
from the British Library.
ISBN 1-903921-57-0
Designed by Abigail Murphy
Published by Autumn House, Grantham, England.
Printed in the USA

Foreword

I warmly welcome and commend Paul Bunday's book of prayers to accompany fifty of the selected group of readings from the Bible. His aim is made clear: 'to help the reader to pray through Scripture – surely a very powerful form of praying. We read it, think about it, absorb it, affirm what it is saying and, finally, turn it into personal prayer.

This aim is abundantly achieved. The chosen themes, including 'Joy in the Lord', 'Beauty of holiness', 'Light conquers darkness', 'Waiting for God', 'No pit so deep', 'Daily work', and 'Lord, you are greater', reveal the writer's rich, reflective spirituality. The prayers, beautifully written, combine a recognition of both the majesty and mercy of the God who has revealed himself supremely in the human face of Jesus Christ. Adoration and gratitude are evoked in response to God's amazing grace. No room for pretence is allowed. Instead, many of the prayers express a refreshing honesty and humility.

Your Word My Prayer will prove to be a great encouragement and stimulus both in private and in public prayer. It will enlarge personal horizons and provide insightful and inspiriting material for church worship and group prayer. Paul Bunday has shared his own journey of Christian discipleship. We are in his debt for helping to illumine and nourish our own daily walk with God.

John Perry

Introduction

It was in 1794 that Samuel Bagster & Sons Ltd first published their *Daily Light on the Daily Path*. Still in print today, it continues to nourish Christians in succeeding generations by assisting them in the habit of regular daily Bible reading. *Daily Light* (as it has become commonly known) has been the inspiration for this book of prayers, and I am indebted to those who first conceived it.

In essence, *Daily Light* does nothing more, or less, than offer the reader a series of themed scripture verses to be used devotionally, morning and evening throughout the year. But therein lies its strength. Because the selected verses are drawn from all over the Bible, they involve the reader in a wide-ranging exploration of God's Word when, all too often, the temptation for many of us is to paddle in the shallows of our favourite and familiar passages.

The intention of *Your Word My Prayer* is to help the reader to pray *through Scripture* – surely, a very powerful form of praying. We start with God's truth – his Word to us. We read it, think about it, absorb it, affirm what it is saying and, finally, turn it into personal prayer. Of course, any prayer can stand on its own, but I believe it will give us confidence in our affirmation and our asking if our prayer is rooted in Scripture.

Generally speaking, the prayers in this book are not a paraphrase of the biblical texts which introduce them.

Your Word *My Prayer*

Rather, they seek to lift the underlying theme from the referenced verse and express it in a way that, hopefully, will enable the user to speak to God in a natural and straightforward manner. Sometimes account has been taken of what readers' aspirations might be, rather than the spiritual experience already enjoyed; in such instances, the prayer is less affirmative, more an honest cry for help (see prayer 29).

In putting together this book of prayers I have for the most part followed selected themes and readings as set out in *Daily Light*; occasionally, changing or reducing the number of its given texts. My aim has been to take the theme of a particular day's reading and use it as a basis for the accompanying prayer.

With one or two exceptions, the prayers are intentionally left open-ended, and without the customary formal ascription; it is to be expected that the biblical texts will 'prime the pump', prompting further - more personal - prayer around the theme in mind.

This book is offered merely as an aid. The reader must have the last word.

Paul Bunday

Contents

Your Word *My Prayer*

Joy in the Lord

Isa. 42:10; Ps. 81:1-2; 40:3; Josh. 1:9;
Neh. 8:10; John 15:5; Rom. 13:11-14

Dear Lord,
You have filled my life with joy
and put a new song in my heart.
If only I could give expression to how I feel about you.
You know there are times
when I feel like singing out loud –
even wishing I could play the trumpet
that I might catch everyone's attention
and tell them how great you are!

Lord, you're the one
who makes me feel like singing.
You're the one who has changed my life.
You're the one who has given me a depth of joy
that makes my friends stop and take notice.
I just pray that the wonderful things you have done in my life
will help others to trust you.

You strengthen and encourage me
in the dark and difficult times of my life:
I have nothing to fear
as I remember your promise to walk with me
every step of the way.

Your Word *My Prayer*

Thank you that your joy brings
so much more than mere happiness –
it gives me a new-found strength and confidence.

And so, dear Lord
help me to keep close to you;
trusting in your power alone,
using my time responsibly,
making the most of every opportunity
you give me to serve you.

As the day of your glorious return
draws ever nearer
help me to clear out of my life
everything that is offensive to you.
Fill me with your light
and I will be able to resist every dark influence
that would subvert me.

Lord Jesus,
you are the Light of the World.
Though darkness seems to be enveloping our society,
your friends on earth do not lose hope.
You have shown us the answer
to the world's pain and problems:
it is to lose ourselves in you.
Covered by your grace
the downward pull of our self-life
will lose its power
so that we can live the way we were meant to
and bring glory to your Name.
Gracious Lord, be glorified in my life this day.

Close to God

John 12:21; Ps. 145:18; Matt. 18:20; 28:20;
Heb. 12:1-2; 1 Cor. 13:12; Phil. 1:23-24; 1 John 3:2-3

Lord Jesus Christ,
as I quietly wait in your presence
open my eyes to see you more clearly.
I really want to get to know you better.

You promised to be close to those
who call upon you with a sincere heart,
so, please, help me to be open and honest before you now.

Thank you for all that I learn about you
as I read your word,
and from those who share their knowledge
and Christian experience with me.
Thank you that we sense your closer presence
when we meet together in your name.

You promised to be with us
even to the end of time – and beyond.
This was your final message
to your friends on earth,
and it seems as if you wanted us
to remember those words above everything.

Lord Jesus, give me the strength
to clear out of my life
anything that might hinder my spiritual growth.

Your Word *My Prayer*

Thank you that you allowed nothing to get in the way
of your saving mission –
even enduring death on a cross –
before taking your rightful place
in the throne room of heaven.
Help me to live each day
with my eyes firmly focused on you,
trusting you every step of the way.

You know there are many times
when I find this difficult:
changing circumstances upset me
and throw me off course.
My life becomes distorted,
my thinking muddled,
and there is so much I don't understand.
Thank you for your assurance
that one day everything will become straight and true
beautiful and whole –
that great day when we will see you face to face
and remain with you for ever.

While I thank you for that vision of future glory
I need your help to live for you *today*.

Though the future is still misty,
completely beyond my imagining,
I thank you that I can live each day
knowing I am a child of my heavenly Father.
I praise you, Lord Jesus
that when you appear in glory
I shall see you as you are
and bear your family likeness.
With such a hope in mind
I want, always, to follow you more closely
and in a way that honours you.

Centre of Everything

Luke 10:40-42; Ps. 42:1&2; Ps. 63:1; Jn. 6:35; Ps. 27:4

Dear Heavenly Father
from the moment I awoke this morning
my mind has been crowded
with all the things I have to do today:
worthwhile things
urgent and important things
necessary things
good things.
My work and responsibilities
cares and concerns
pleasures and interests
all jostle for position in claiming my attention.
The Martha in me takes over
even before I've had breakfast!
Slow me down, dear Lord
rein me in.
Draw me with the magnet of your love
back to the centre and focus of my faith.
Turn my eyes upon you
that I may see your glory
and seek that better part –
yourself alone.

Then will my heart delight
in a joy far beyond
anything that this world can offer.

Your Word *My Prayer*

Living Lord
just as a hunted animal longs
to quench its thirst
in the cooling water of the stream
so my dry soul longs for the refreshment
that can be found only in yourself.

You are Creator of the Universe
and yet you call me into
a close, personal relationship with yourself.
You are my God
and I long for you:
in a world which all too often
disappoints and depresses me
you alone can truly satisfy my heart-felt yearning.

I call to mind the words of Jesus:
I am the Bread of Life
and I know that he alone can satisfy
my deepest spiritual need.

I pray that I may daily feed upon him
learning from Mary of Bethany
to sit quietly at your feet
listening to you
delighting in your word
and drinking the joy of your presence.

The sum total of all my desire
is to feel at home in your company
every day of my life.
Draw me ever closer to yourself
that I may see the beauty of your holiness
and meditate upon your glorious perfection.

See you more clearly

Luke 18:41; Ps. 119:18; Luke 24:45; John 14:26;
Eph. 1:17-20; Rom. 8:37

Loving Jesus,
how readily you answered
the heart-felt cry of the blind man –
restoring his sight
revealing to him the wonders of your creation.

I ask you today for the gift of inward vision
that will enable me to understand
the wonder of your word to me in the Scriptures.

Long ago, you drew near and fell into step
with those two disciples on the Emmaus road.
You explained the Scriptures to them
opening their spiritual eyes
and warming their hearts with your truth.
Lord, please do the same for me now.

Today, I take hold of your promise
that the Holy Spirit will be my teacher.
Help me to trust that, like a good friend,
he will patiently explain anything I don't understand,

helping me to remember
those vital lessons you taught your followers
while you were still on earth.

Dear Lord, open my eyes
to see more of your glory and wonder.
Give me a fresh insight into the hope of my calling
and help me to appreciate more fully
the heavenly inheritance I share with all who trust in you.
Most of all, I pray
that you will open my eyes to the greatness of your power:
that same mighty power which raised you
from the darkness of death
into glorious new life.

Help me to praise you for this great truth
as I find myself lifted up daily, hourly,
into your resurrection life –
to become *'more than a conqueror'*
through your love.

Thanks be to Thee, my Lord Jesus Christ,
For all the pains and insults you have borne for me,
And for all the benefits you have won for me.
O most merciful Redeemer, friend and brother,
May I see you more clearly
Love you more dearly
And follow you more nearly
Day by day. Amen.
(Prayer of Richard of Chichester)

Best of friends

Prov. 18:24; Exod. 33:11; John 15:14,15; Luke 17:10;
Rom. 8:15,16; Phil. 4:6; Prov. 15:8

Lord God,
as I bring to mind the friends whom I love and value,
I thank you for the joy I have in knowing them.

I thank you most of all
for friendship with yourself.
Draw me into a closer relationship with you
so that I can know something
of the privilege that Moses enjoyed –
of speaking to you face-to-face as a friend.

Your word tells me that
those who trust and obey you
are counted as your friends,
and you share your plans with them.
Help me to be more perceptive:
open my eyes to see where your Spirit is at work.
Then I will be able to play my part –
either through prayer, or in offering
my time or gifts in your service
I want to be useful to you.

Your Word *My Prayer*

Never let me forget that even when I try
to serve you to the best of my ability
I've done no more than my duty:
I could never repay the debt
of your undeserved love for me.

But you are a God of grace and
you freely give me your Holy Spirit.
He assures me that,
as your son or daughter,
I can call you *Father, dear Father.*

In that trusting relationship
help me to bring every part of my life into prayer.
As I make my personal requests to you,
and remember the needs of others,
don't ever let me forget to thank you.

Keep me from taking your good gifts for granted:
I know that it is your delight
to receive the praise of all who trust you,
so I praise and thank you right now
for all the many blessings I enjoy
through your grace and goodness:
I call them to mind
in gratitude and thanksgiving . . . .

Because he first loved us

1 Peter 1:8; 1 John 4:16, 19; Eph. 1:12-13;
Col. 1:27; 1 John 4:20; Ps. 150:6

Lord Jesus Christ,
when I am tempted to wish I had seen you
face to face, as your disciples did,
let my desire rather be
to walk by faith, not sight
yet still to love you as they loved you.

I know I can never hope to do this
until I fully understand
how much you love me –
and always have:
yes, even before I had any knowledge of you,
let alone thoughts of loving you!

Lord Jesus, you have revealed to me
the heart of my Father God.
Only through you
could I have come to know
that *God is love*, and that
to live in him is to live in love.

Thank you for those first disciples
who faithfully shared the good news
of your saving love.
Thank you that we who trust in you
are guaranteed by your Holy Spirit
to belong to you for ever.

Thank you for the glorious good news
that your salvation is offered to all.
We who live in you rejoice in the hope
of sharing your glory.

Lord, you measure the sincerity of my love for you
by my attitude to other people.
Help me to remember this
when I have hostile feelings towards anyone.
Help me to demonstrate my love for you
by my patient acceptance of other people.
Thank you so much for accepting
and loving me.

Loving Lord, I praise you
for your grace and goodness.
May all your people praise you
for you alone are worthy!

Lead me, Lord

Ps. 48:14; 23:2-4; 73:23-26; 33:21; 138:8;
Isa. 25:1; Phil. 1:6

Loving Heavenly Father,
the deeply satisfying relationship I enjoy with you
influences every aspect of my life.
How wonderful to know
that your guiding hand
will direct my path
all the days of my time on this earth
and even into eternity.

You are my God:
I honour your name.
I praise you for
all your good and wonderful plans for me:
for every good purpose
you are bringing to fruition in my life.
I feel so privileged.

Thank you
for programming in quiet periods
of rest and relaxation,
when I can feed my spirit
and gather strength
to keep travelling the path
you have mapped out for me.
When I feel uneasy
and heavy-hearted,

Your Word *My Prayer*

when I fear for life itself,
your presence comforts me.
Knowing I'm held in your strong hand
helps me to overcome all my fears.
As you lead me onward,
your close companionship
gives me all-round protection.

As I live in your presence,
held by your hand,
you constantly lead me onwards,
blessing me with your wise guidance.
As long as I am with you
in this life and the next,
there is nothing more I would ask.
Here on earth you fill my every horizon.
Even if all human resources fail, Lord,
keep me believing that you are
totally sufficient for all my needs.

How glad I am to know you, Lord
and trust in your saving name.

Thank you that I can be confident
that you will fulfil
your purpose and plan for my life;
that your constant love assures me
of the final, happy outcome.

Please don't let me fail you
through any weakness on my part;
keep me trusting that
just as you have begun a good work in me
so you will complete it
by the day of Christ's return.

Beauty of holiness

2 Chron. 3:18; 20:21; Ezek. 16:14; Ps. 128:1-2;
Prov.16:3; Phil. 2:12-13; 2 Thess. 2:16-17

Father God,
help me to worship you
in the beauty of holiness, so that your holiness
might be reflected in my life –
however faintly.

Your beauty radiates throughout the world,
transforming all who trust in Jesus.
May the light of your glory change me
more and more into his likeness.
Help me to remember that this can only happen
when I open up my life
to your Holy Spirit.

May I experience more of your joy
as I seek to honour you
and walk in your way.
I want my life to be beautiful and useful –
producing the fruit of the Spirit.
I know that this is only possible
if I am deeply rooted in Jesus.

Your Word *My Prayer*

And so I commit this day to you,
trusting you to guide me and help me
in all that I have to do.

Help me always to live in the light of the salvation
which Jesus has won for me.
May I humbly and reverently
direct all the divine energy you give me
towards those things which please you most.
Please give me the perseverance
to finish the work you call me to.

Because of your amazing grace
I am secure in the love of Jesus.
and can be confident that all will be well.
Living in this hope, and trusting in your power,
must surely influence everything
I say and do this day.
I'm so glad that you are in charge.

Privileged
access

James 4:8; Luke 24:15; Ps. 73:28; 2 Chron. 15:2,4;
Jer. 29:11-13; Heb.10:19-22; Rom. 8:37

God above all,
what an amazing privilege you have given me –
nothing less than access
to the throne room of heaven!
Right now, I can approach you with confidence
because Jesus died for me.
He has broken down the barrier
through his victorious death on the cross.
I praise you that the way is now open
for me to enter freely into your holy presence –
and all because I have been made clean
by the blood of Jesus.

Dear Heavenly Father,
I am resting in your promise
that as I get close to you
you will move in beside me.

Your word tells me that you desire
to walk with your friends;
So I believe that
you delight to come alongside *me*
the moment I share my need
or my loneliness with you.

Your Word My Prayer

It's so good to know
that you are close to me right now;
so good to feel secure in your presence.
Help me to find the words
to share this blessing with others,
drawing them, too, into the orbit of your love.

Thank you that you are always there for me.
Forgiving me for those times
when I have walked away from you,
thinking I could manage on my own.
And thank you that when I do wander off
you are always ready to take me back
the moment I admit I can't make it without you.

Everything you plan for me is good:
you think only of my welfare.
Your ear is tuned to my faintest cry:
every stumbling prayer is heard by you.
Thank you for your promise
that I will surely find you
when I seek you with a sincere heart.

Thank you that as I live in the peace
which Jesus has won for me
I can know his victory in my life:
keep me resting always
in your love.

Forgiving *spirit*

Eph. 4:26; Matt. 18:15; Matt. 18:21-22;
Mark 11:25; Col. 3:12-13; Eph. 4:32

Gracious Lord,
I come to you today because
sometimes I have a problem controlling my anger.
I flare up and overreact
and then say words I bitterly regret.
I tell myself that it's just human nature
but really there's no excuse.
Forgive me when I have allowed angry exchanges
to fester in my mind day after day.
When I've been in the wrong
give me the humility to admit it
and do my best to put things right.
When I feel that another has hurt me
help me not to bear a grudge.

If ever a serious difference threatens
to cause a breakdown in relationship with someone,
help me to bring it into the open
so we can talk it through together –
openly, honestly
and in confidence.

Some times I feel aggrieved,
remembering that I've been down this road so often.
Why should I keep on forgiving,
when the same thing keeps happening?

Your Word *My Prayer*

When I get hurt again and again?
It's not fair;
enough is enough.
But what is enough?
Six, seven times?
Not in your book, Lord –
Jesus tells me there is no upper limit
to forgiveness.
I have only to look at the cross to know that.

Thank you for reminding me
how much I have been forgiven,
and that I must pass that forgiveness on to others.
Your pardon must come full circle:
it starts with you
and returns to you.

In your love,
you have chosen me and given me a new life:
you want the very best for me.
Help me to clothe myself
in the gracious garments you provide
to cover my deficiencies:
compassion, kindness, humility, patience.
Help me at all times
to live in harmony with others.
I can have no greater motivation to forgive another
than the recollection of the great debt
the Lord Jesus has cancelled in my own life.

I pray that your Holy Spirit will help me –
always – to be kind and warm-hearted to others:
constantly ready to forgive
as I have been forgiven by you.

Lift me, Lord

Ps. 119:25; Col. 3:1-3; Phil. 3:20-21; Gal. 5:17;
Rom. 8:12-13; 1 Peter 2:11

Heavenly Father,
When I remember
how you raised Jesus up out of death,
I know that you can do the same for me.
When I'm feeling negative and depressed,
help me to trust you to lift me in spirit
to where Christ sits with you in glory.
Since I have died with Christ
and my life is now caught up in him,
I ask you to help me keep my mind
focused on heaven,
that wonderful place where
my life is now registered!
Thank you for the expectation
of all that is to come –
there is so much to look forward to.
Thank you that Jesus will return
to transform my hopes into realities
and to change my weak, failing body
to resemble his glorified body.
Thank you that he has the power
to carry out his perfect plan.

Your Word *My Prayer*

Lord, as you can see,
you've lifted my eyes to the glorious future.
But now I'm brought down to earth with a bang
as I remember the constant struggle
to keep my lower nature in check.
It seems to be at war with your Spirit,
pulling me in the opposite direction.
No wonder I have difficulty doing your will.

Father, help me to see the real issue here –
that my lower nature
no longer has any claim on me.
Never let me excuse my wrongdoing by saying:
'It's only human nature.'
Your word tells me
it doesn't have to be like that.
Your Holy Spirit can make me victorious
over all the destructive influences
which would control me.

Help me to remember
that my real home is in heaven,
and that in this life
I must expect to have conflict.
Give me strength to resist evil
and put your will above my own selfish desire.

Promised
Presence

Deut. 31:8; Exod. 33:14-15; Matt. 28:20;
Ps. 37:23-24; 73:23-24; Rom. 8:38-39

Father of all,
I cannot know exactly
what this day holds for me,
but I thank you for your promise
to go before me in all that I do.
It is so reassuring to remember
that you are with me
and will never fail me.

I know that without your help
I could never accomplish anything worthwhile.
Left to myself, I'd be sure to go off in at a tangent,
rather than sticking to your way of doing things.
I don't want to go through
this – or any – day without you.

Day by day, help me to rest
in that last great promise of Jesus
to be with us always – even to the end of time.

When I live each day with my eyes fixed on you,
I know it brings joy to your heart.
When I turn aside from you I fail,
and yet you still love me!

Your Word *My Prayer*

When I fall you pick me up
and set me straight again.
Thank you for your strong supporting arm.

You never stop loving me;
every day I am in your presence,
and you guide me with your wise advice.
I know that one day you will receive me
into that glorious new home
you are preparing, and that
I will be with you forever.

That means I can face this day confidently,
as I trust myself to you
for all that is to come.
No circumstances in my life –
today or tomorrow –
no earthly powers,
no demonic forces –
nothing in the whole of creation –
can ever separate me from your love, dear Father,
the love shown to us in Jesus Christ our Lord.

Secret of

fruitfulness

Ps. 92:12-14; 104:16; Hos. 14:5-6; Jer. 17:7-8

Creator God,
thank you for the changing seasons
which speak to us of your loving and controlling hand
upon our earth.
Thank you for the beauty of trees that come into bud
as the dark days of winter give way to Spring
and all is fresh and green again –
evidence of your renewing love
and resurrection power.

The rising sap that nourishes the new growth
speaks to us of your life-giving Spirit.
Thank you for your promise to your people of old
that you would be as the refreshing dew to them –
beautifying, strengthening,
firmly rooting and making fruitful:
a fragrant witness to you,
their saving God.

Those who trust you completely
bask in your favour:
their spiritual life remains strong and healthy.
They are like trees planted beside a river
whose leaves stay fresh and green
even when a scorching heat-wave
shrivels up everything around them.
Father God, I want my life to be fruitful.
Keep me firmly rooted in you,
and help me to trust in you alone.
Thank you for your promise
to nourish and renew all who abide in you:
thank you that your springs of living water
never run dry.

Today I want to live in your promise
that all who trust in you
will flourish like palm trees
and grow in stature as the cedars of Lebanon:
they will be joyful in worship
and privileged to serve you –
even through to the last years of their life.
Thank you, Father
for this beautiful picture from your word.
Help me to keep it in mind;
it's how I want my life to be.

Fellowship

Mal. 3:16; Luke 24:15; Matt. 12:36-37; 18:20;
Col. 3:16; Heb. 3:13; Phil. 4:2-3

Lord Jesus Christ,
I thank you for the joy of Christian fellowship;
the way we are able to encourage one another
by our word of testimony.
When our conversation is all of you
we know that you listen attentively,
and, yes, our words are actually noted in heaven!

Your risen presence is
the secret of our joy:
you are constantly drawing near to us –
in our working,
walking and talking . . .
as we relax in other believers' homes,
or simply enjoy being quiet together . . .
you are right there in the midst of us –
just as you promised you'd be with your friends
whenever they meet in your Name.

Your word teaches us
the importance of meeting together:
it gives us the opportunity to worship you
and give expression to our joy.
It is the means by which we encourage
and build one another up.
Help us to be sensitive to those

struggling with doubts
or confused in their belief.
Give us grace and wisdom as we seek
to keep each other
firmly on course.

Help us to feel responsible for each other,
and be prepared to speak up
if we sense a spiritual problem,
but always doing so with
kindness and humility.

May we think before we speak:
our words can build up and encourage,
but they can also be destructive.
Every careless expression,
every thoughtless word, will be noted
and must be answered for to you.
Forgive us when we have failed
to control our tongues
and hurt others with our words.
Be in our speaking –
Be in my speaking –
that all my words may be gracious and truthful.

When disputes flare up
and fellowship is endangered
may I do all in my power
to settle differences quickly.
So that, as I work together to further your cause,
I can ever rejoice that my name
is enrolled in your heavenly register.

Peace
beyond
understanding

John 20:19; 1 Thess. 5:23; 2 Thess. 2:16,17;
Phil. 4:7; Eph. 2:14; 1 Cor. 1:8

God of peace,
when my life is in turmoil
speak to me the words of the risen Jesus
to his devastated friends:
'Peace be with you.'
I need to hear your word of peace to me now.

May that peace permeate my life today
at every level -
quietening my mind,
calming my emotions,
setting me on an even keel.
Thank you that your purpose for us is wholeness of life
in which we can experience
your divine peace.

Your Word *My Prayer*

Please grant me that peace
which passes all understanding.
Your word encourages me to believe
that this is your desire for me:
open my life to receive your gift of peace
that it may guard my mind and spirit.
When I lose the sense of your peace
it may be because I have wandered from you:
At such times, send me signs that will alert me
to move back into the centre of your will –
into your welcoming presence,
where there is tranquillity and harmony.

Thank you, dear Father,
that you love me
in Jesus your Son.
I can enjoy true peace through him
for he is my peace.
Keep your love fresh in my mind
so that I may share your peace
with those who are troubled or unhappy.

New every morning

Ps. 41:3; 46:10; Lam. 3:22-23; Deut. 33:25; Mal. 4:2;
Exod. 15 :26; Matt. 8:17; Rom. 8:28; Isa. 49:15

Loving heavenly Father,
at the start of this new day
you want nothing more than to have me with you,
quietly resting in your presence.
You are speaking in the silence
assuring me that you are the living God.
Here before you
I touch base . . .
I engage with reality . . .
I seek your blessing . . .

Every morning
your endless mercies are showered upon me
your compassionate love embraces me.
How utterly reliable are your promises.
Great is your faithfulness!

Thank you, Father,
that I can be sure
you will uphold me till the very end:
even age and infirmity

Your Word *My Prayer*

will not hamper your purpose for my life
because you will always strengthen me
to do all that you require of me.

Father, I pray for those
who feel that their physical strength is ebbing:
those who are wearied by pain,
worn down by anxiety,
enfeebled by great age.
I picture them in my mind
as I bring them into your presence . . .
Help them to trust you
and to know that your healing wings
are overshadowing them.

For you are our healer;
you are the one who makes us truly whole.

Thank you, Father
that you are our divine physician.
Draw close and minister
to all who are confined to bed:
sustain them in their weakness
and deliver them from all
that distresses and discomforts them.

Throughout the busyness
and pressures of this day
We may forget you;
but how I thank you, Father God,
that you never – for a single moment –
forget us.

Jesus our peace

Eph. 2:14; 2 Cor. 5:19-21; Col. 1:14, 20-22;
Eph. 2:15; John 14:17

Dear God of peace,
you have shown your people how to find true peace.
Thank you so much that this is something
we don't have to strive for.
Your word tells us that Jesus himself is our peace
and he freely gives himself to us
when we reach out to him.

Thank you, dear Father,
that you were united in your Son
as he suffered on the cross,
bringing us back into fellowship with you
by removing the sin and blame from our lives.
Thank you that we need never doubt
that our friendship with you has been restored,
because all the rubbish in our lives
was taken into Jesus' sinless life
and totally destroyed when he died.
Through his sacrifice for us,
we were put right with you –
yes, every last sin washed away!

Thank you, that the way is now open
for all heaven and earth

to be united with you;
and all because Jesus has made peace between us
through his willing sacrifice.
Once we were alienated from you,
separated from you by our sins,
and totally turned in upon ourselves;
but Jesus has changed everything.
He has taken
every dark and evil act or thought
into his calvary sacrifice of faith and love,
making it possible for us to live
beautiful and blameless lives.

What wonderful peace comes from knowing
that all charges against us are dismissed,
every penalty set aside,
every debt cancelled,
every sin forgiven!

Jesus, our peace,
unifies and harmonises
all the discordant forces in the world,
making it possible for us
to live in peace with one another.
And so your Kingdom grows.
Thank you, dear Father.

May the peace which Jesus bequeathed to us
be our daily experience,
and as we live in your presence
may it be the air we breathe,
banishing fear and quietening our hearts
in a way that the world can never believe is possible
until it encounters Jesus himself.

Without *fault* before *God*

Hab. 1:13; 1 John 2:1-2; Jer. 50:20; Micah 7:18-19;
Eph. 1:6; Col. 1:21-22; Jude 24-25

O God of purity and light,
in your perfect holiness
you can never condone the sins of your children,
so you cannot overlook my sin.
How it must grieve your loving heart
to see the suffering I bring upon myself and others
through the misuse of my free will.

However hard I try, I still fail you –
offending against your laws
and hurting other people.
How I thank you, gracious Father,
that there is a way for me
to be put right with you again.
Thank you for Jesus,
who gave his life for my sin,
who stands in your presence
and speaks up for me.

Your Word *My Prayer*

Thank you, dear Father,
for your promise of forgiveness.
Your grace was revealed to your chosen people of old.
Yes, even when they rebelled against you
you kept your pledge to the faithful remnant.

Who can compare with you, O Lord?
I stand in awe of the amazing mercy
you have shown to your people all through the ages
and the redeeming love that reaches us today.
How can I ever praise you enough for your compassion
as you forgive me over and over again?
You remove my sins from me:
you tread them under your feet
setting me free from guilt and shame.
Who can compare with you, O Lord?

Mindful of all that you have done for me, dear Father,
I am confident that you can keep me safe
until that day when I stand before you
and see you, face to face, in all your glory.

Father, dear Father

John 17:1,11, 25; Mark 14:36; Rom. 8:15; Gal. 4:6;
Eph. 2:18-19; Luke 15:18-24

Dearest Father,
thank you for the wonderful revelation
Jesus gives us in his praying.
On the night before he died,
when he had finished supper with his friends,
he prayed to you:
Father . . . Holy Father . . . Righteous Father . . .

Holy and righteous you are, Lord God.
And yet, when your Son
went into the garden of Gethsemane
to pour out his heart to you in prayer,
he called you by that most intimate
and affectionate name:
Abba, Father.

And now, dear Father
I, too, may come to you in prayer
addressing you as *Abba*,
because your word tells me I may.
How wonderful to know
that you have adopted me into your family;
what confidence this gives me,
to use such an intimate
and personal form of address.

Your Word *My Prayer*

Indeed, your Holy Spirit within me
encourages me to call you
Abba, Father.
Your love is beyond words:
may I never take it for granted.

I praise you, Father
that the door to you is wide open
and all because of Jesus.
In him, I may now come to you
through your Holy Spirit.
And yet more! Even those who once
thought they were not eligible
are now included in your one great family
with the full citizen rights
of all who follow Jesus!

Sometimes I wander away from you:
squandering your gifts,
wasting my time,
selfishly doing my own thing.
When I come to my senses I recall your fatherly love:
I look for words to explain myself –
and then I remember
I can still come to you as your child
and call you *Abba.*
No way do I deserve that amazing privilege
but when I return to you
I find such a welcome:
your loving embrace,
the covering robe,
the covenant ring –
all that signifies that I am still
your beloved child.

Casting
care
upon
him

Isa. 12:2; 26:3; 30:15; Ps. 55:22; Matt. 8:26;
Phil. 4:6-7; John 14:27

Precious Lord,
your peace is the most precious gift
I can possess.
With your peace in my heart
I am able to appreciate and enjoy
all the good things of life.
Help me to keep my mind centred in you,
so that in quiet trust I may be fully open
to receive your perfect peace.

When troubles arise
help me to hand them over to you
that I may experience your sustaining power.
You promise to fail me never.

No wonder I can rejoice!
You are my strength and my song.
You dissolve away all my fears.

Your Word *My Prayer*

Forgive me when I am so preoccupied with my problems
that I forget you are with me.
Instead of trusting you
I become more and more worked up
as I struggle to keep my head above water.
Only you can calm the storm and restore my peace.

Your Word tells me not to worry about anything
but to bring my concerns to you in prayer.
May I never forget to thank you
for the many times in the past
when you listened to my troubles and helped me.
Recalling your goodness
will drive away negative thoughts and fears
and allow your peace to flow in.

Thank you for the assurance
that when I am in a right relationship with you -
quietly trusting
prayerfully waiting -
you will strengthen me
and save me.

Search me and Try me

Lam. 3:40; Ps. 26:2; 51:6; 139:7,15-16; Rom. 3:23;
1 John 1:9; 1 John 2:1-2; Heb. 10:19-22

Holy Father,
help me today
to take an honest look at my life:
to examine and test
not only my outward words and actions
but the secret thoughts and motives that prompt them.

Let your spirit probe me
at every level of consciousness.

I know that you look for
sincerity of heart,
so help me to unravel my twisted thoughts.
Show me if my spring of life
is polluted at its source.

Your presence is inescapable;
I can never hide from you.
You know me through and through.
From the moment of my conception
you traced every part of my development.
Just like a proud parent
you never missed a thing
as you lovingly watched
each stage of my growth,
every turning point in my life.

Your Word *My Prayer*

All my days are recorded in your book.

Oh Father, how I've let you down.
When I'm in your holy presence
I feel really bad about myself.
But I come back to you today,
joyfully claiming those amazing promises
which sound almost too good to be true.
But yes, I *know* I can trust you:
when I confess my sin and failure
you forgive me, and heal me
of all that has gone wrong in my life.

My confidence is in Jesus
your holy, righteous Son.
He speaks up for me in heaven.
He is the friend who stands by
those he died to save.

What a turn-around
that brings about for fallen humanity!
Now I can have confidence to come
right into your holy presence.
Jesus has opened up the way to you
through his life, death and glorious resurrection.
Now I can picture him,
my friend, my great high priest,
praying for me in heaven.
Help me now to draw near to you
with a clear conscience,
trusting myself to the grace of my Lord Jesus Christ
and all he has done for me.
I truly believe
that he has taken full responsibility for me.
Keep me firm in this wonderful hope
you have given me in him.

True  rest

Deut. 12:9; Heb. 4:9; 6:19-20; John 14:2-3;
Rev. 21:4; Matt. 6:20; Col. 3:2-3

Dearest Lord,
It has been wisely said:
*'You have made us for yourself
and our hearts are restless till they find their rest in you.'*
You know how I long for that rest
and yet how often it eludes me.
All too often I leave you out of the equation
and try to sort out my problems for myself,
striving – when I could be resting
worrying – when I should be trusting;
times that leave me frustrated
and ever more restless.

In your love you gave your people of old a Sabbath rest.
You knew how much they needed respite from their labour
and time to worship you.
You know how much we still need that today.
May I always be grateful for your day
and use it as you intended.
There are many who do not have that luxury:
those engaged in vital services to our community,
those with demanding domestic responsibilities,
those who, for whatever reason,
find it hard to be part of a worshipping community.
Refresh and strengthen them by your Spirit, Lord.

Your Word *My Prayer*

Thank you that your special day points us forward
to that eternal rest
which you have prepared for us in the life to come.

My hope is anchored in Jesus,
who has already entered into
that eternal resting place.
I thank you that he holds out to me
a life-line which draws me into your presence:
there alone can I find true peace.

I come back to you now,
to find my rest in Jesus.
I look forward to that heavenly resting place
which Jesus has prepared –
where there is room for everyone
to be at home with him, for ever.
Comfort and strengthen today
all who mourn the loss of loved ones. . .
those who have nowhere on earth to call their home . . .
those who are dying alone and afraid.
May they rest in the promise of Jesus,
that where he is we shall also be:
with him – for ever.

How this hope encourages me
in times of trouble and uncertainty.
The best is yet to be!
Thank you that you have promised
a bright and glorious future,
when you will make all things new.
You will wipe away all tears,
because in that new life
you will have abolished sorrow and pain –
even death itself.
That will be peace as we have never known it.

The offence
of the
Cross

Matt. 16:24; James 4:4; Acts 14:22; Rom. 9:33;
1 Peter 2:7-8; Gal. 2:20; 5:24; 6:14; 2 Tim. 2:12

Lord Jesus Christ,
I thank you for the joy that comes
from following you.
Help me to accept that this means
walking in the shadow of your cross.
Your word teaches me
that there are two crosses I must welcome:
Calvary's cross
on which you died, bearing my sin,
that I might be made righteous and acceptable to God
through faith in you.
Then there is the personal cross,
which I must accept
as I follow you daily.

Your Word *My Prayer*

You gave your friends fair warning
that they could expect trouble
if they embraced your cause.
Even today, in some parts of your world
there are those suffering greatly for their faith.
Strengthen those who have to bear
such a heavy cross.
Help me cheerfully to accept
the minor slights and criticisms
that my own Christian witness may invite.
May I never compromise with the world's values
for the sake of living a comfortable life.
How could I count myself as your friend
if I did such a thing?

I know I must expect
opposition from time to time.
May we who love you encourage one another
to keep faith in times of difficulty.

Thank you that I never need to be ashamed
of my faith in you!
You are infinitely precious to me.

Everlasting Love

Ps. 16:5-6; 63:1,5-7; 73:25-26; 119:11;
Num 18:20; Lam. 3:24; Jer. 31:3

Lord of the morning,
I am coming to you today
simply for the joy of being in your presence.
You are my dear heavenly Father:
you are all I need.

Only you can satisfy my deepest longing.
No one on earth
nor in heaven itself
means more to me than you.
My life may fall apart
but you are my rock of support
that can never fail.
You are the mainspring,
the very centre of my life.

Your Word *My Prayer*

You are my first choice:
I'm committed to you for life.
You hold the title deeds
of my very existence.
What a wonderful inheritance I'm enjoying
in the security of your love.
How pleasant it is to walk trustingly
along the paths you have chosen for me.

My future is secure in your safe hands
my hope focused on you alone.
ThIs is my rich inheritance
my priceless treasure:
you are mine and I am yours
for ever.

God's answers

Job 3:23-26; 38:1; Isa. 37:14-15; 65.24; Luke 22:40-43;
Gen. 18:4; Ps. 37:5; Phil. 4:6; Rom. 8:26

Lord of all hopefulness,
thank you for all that your word in scripture
teaches me about the priceless gift of prayer.

Help me to learn from Job to be honest with you.
When he was in the agony of overwhelming misfortune
he opened his heart to you,
pouring out his grief and bitterness,
and you heard him.
You patiently reasoned with him,
and eventually restored him.
You poured out such bountiful blessing upon him
and more than made up for all his suffering.

Help me to learn from Hezekiah,
to bring every anxiety before you;
the phone call that disturbs me,
the letter that brings bad news,
the hospital appointment that weighs on my mind,
the family concerns that rob me of sleep . . . . .
May I always affirm your lordship
over every circumstance of my life.

Draw near to those who are filled with dread . . .
tormented with anguish . . .
racked with pain . . .

Your Word *My Prayer*

comfort and strengthen those I am bringing to mind
and make them victorious through your saving power.
Thank you for the peace that Jesus won for us
through his obedience to your will.

Almighty Father, never let me forget
that nothing is too hard for you.
Your power and your love are unbounded.

Teach me to come to you at the start of each day
offering you my work, my plans, my hopes;
trusting you to guide me
and keep me in your will.

What a wonderful encouragement you have given us
in your promise to answer our prayers.
Before we've barely uttered the words
you are coming to our help!

Dear Father, you want so much
for your children to be free of worry:
to unburden themselves to you in prayer.
May I learn to bring every anxious fear to you,
confident of your loving concern,
your power to help.
And may I never forget to thank you.

When I find it hard to pray,
when my thoughts are confused,
when I don't know where to start,
or how to express myself . . .
remind me that your Holy Spirit prays within me,
interpreting my stumbling words,
and winging my heart-felt longings to your throne of grace.
What greater encouragement can we have to pray?

Light conquers darkness

Job 7:4; Ps. 30:4-5; Heb. 10:37; 2 Sam. 23:4;
John 14:2-3; 27-28; 1 Thess. 5:5; Rev. 21:25

Lord of day and night,
my life, at times, seems like
one of those fretful, sleepless nights
in which I toss and turn through the dark hours,
all the while longing for the dawn.

Only you can forgive my sins,
lifting me from my sorrow, guilt and shame.
May I never doubt
that just as day follows night,
so the light of your presence
is able to disperse the doubts and fears
which overshadow my life from time to time.

Help me to be patient,
trusting completely in your perfect timing.

Your Word *My Prayer*

You are as the light of morning;
you dispel the darkness
and renew me with fresh hope.

Forgive my feeble faith –
the fears about the future
that spring to mind in times of uncertainty.
Fill me with your peace,
that I may rest in the promise
that Jesus is surely coming back for us.

As a child of the light
I want to live in the light as my natural element.
Help me to live each day
with the sunshine of your love,
radiating into every part of my life –
body, mind and spirit.

Thank you, Lord,
that there is no night in the heavenly home;
darkness has been vanquished
and the light of your love reigns for ever.

# God of
faithfulness

Josh. 1:5; 21:45; Num. 23:19; Deut. 7:9;
Isa. 49:15-16; Zeph. 3:17

Father God,
when I feel that my strength
Is not equal to the tasks
and responsibilities of this day,
help me to remember Joshua.
You promised to guide and help him
every day of his life.

Every single thing you promised
you faithfully brought to pass.
You never once let him down.

I thank you, Father,
that your word to us is utterly trustworthy.
In our flawed human nature
we break our promises
and go back on our word,
but you would never ever do such a thing.

Your promises are reliable,
your everlasting covenant unbreakable:
great is your faithfulness
to those who trust and obey you.

The beautiful sight of a mother
breast-feeding her baby
wonderfully demonstrates the deep bond
and security of mother-love.
Yet, sadly, even mothers can fail their children.
How I praise and thank you
that your love for us is unchanging and for ever:
you will *never* forget us:
you tell us that our individual names
are written on the palms of your hands!

I thank you that your promised presence
is always where we need you most:
you are constantly on hand
and ready to help us.
You keep us safe
and give us victory in times of trouble.
More and more, may I learn
to rest back in your love.
Even now, I pray that you will open my ears
to catch the echoes of the heavenly choir
singing of your joy in your children –
yes, even in me.
Great is your faithfulness!

Pruned for fruitfulness

John 15:1-2; Mal. 3:2-3; Heb. 5:8; 12:7-8, 11-12;
Rom. 5:3-5

Lord,
I have to admit
there are times when I don't warm to your word.
I like the bit about fruitful lives –
but I'm not so keen
on the pruning part of the process.

Again, I like the thought
of being as pure gold in your service –
but I recoil from the purifying fire
that needs to do its refining work in my life.
But you tell me that
this is the way it works:
pruning, purifying.
It has to be done.
Help me to accept it.

Never let me forget the example of Jesus:
he learned obedience through suffering.
If that was needful in his experience
there can surely be no short cuts for me.

Your Word *My Prayer*

Help me to view my problems and trials
in a more positive light –
even as something that can be creative.
Help me to believe that endurance
will teach me to be patient;
this, in turn, will strengthen my character
and increase my trust in you.
Your Holy Spirit warms my heart,
flooding my whole being
with the assurance of your love for me
so that I never lose hope,
whatever may happen.
Lord, there is another aspect
of thls pruning and purifying process.
You are treating me as a wise, concerned parent
would treat a much loved child.
Help me to see this as a privilege,
and in no way a punishment.
In your loving wisdom
you know exactly
where I need reshaping and reforming
to be more useful in your service.

May I look beyond
the painful discipline of the present moment
to the new maturity
you wish to develop in me.
From now on help me to submit
to your way of doing things
and may I go out to serve you this day
with a new enthusiasm and expectancy.

He is *able*

2 Tim. 1:12; Eph. 3:20; Gen. 18:14; 2 Cor. 9:8;
Heb. 7:25; Jude 24

Dear Heavenly Father,
help me today to lay hold of
that great lesson of faith:
you are a God *who is able!*
You are able
to bring me through every difficulty,
to overcome every obstacle,
to keep me safe right to the end.
Persuade my wavering mind that
you are bigger than any of my problems;
you are the higher power,
greater than any other human or spiritual authority.

My prayers, my desires,
my hopes and aspirations,
don't come within a million miles
of what you can do for me!
Help me to believe
that you are able to do so much more
than I could ever ask or imagine,
through your mighty power
at work in my life.

Really, there is nothing –
absolutely nothing –
that you cannot do!

Your Word *My Prayer*

Help me to trust in your promise
that the more freely I give,
the more you will bless me.
You not only make it up to me,
you leave me so much
better off than I was before!

What a joy it is to know
that you are able to save completely
all who come to you through Jesus.
I thank you, Father, that at this moment –
and for ever –
he is praying for us,
pleading his death on our behalf.

I praise you
that you are able
to keep me from falling.
You will uphold me to the end:
until that day when
I stand in your glorious presence
without a stain on my character.

Until then, please help me
to keep faith with you,
even if I have to endure
opposition and unpopularity.
I'm committed to you for life
because I know I can trust you.
I am confident that you are able to take care of me,
and all that I'm trying to do in your name,
right to the end of my life.

Conflict and compromise

Num. 33:55; Rev. 3:16; 1 Tim. 6:12; 2 Cor. 10:4-5;
Rom. 7:23; 8:12-13; Gal. 5:17-18; John 19:30

Father God,
you have warned your people of the dangers of
a self-indulgent life,
a half-hearted discipleship,
a lukewarm love for you.

You freely offer all of yourself to us
and yet we still hold back from you:
we find it hard to go all the way
in Christian commitment.

Help us to be mindful that we are engaged
in spiritual warfare,
and to trust in your help at all times.

Stick close to us when we find ourselves
in the thick of the battle against your truth.
Help us to hold on to our Christian principles,
and strengthen us in our struggle
against the subtle influence of the world.
Our human resources are useless.
but you have given us spiritual weapons
so that we may confidently face every evil power.
Thus armed and protected,
we may seek to overcome every obstacle
to the spread of your kingdom.

Your Word *My Prayer*

Thank you that we don't have to live
at the level of our lower nature –
in weakness, failure and defeat.
That way of life leads to a dead end.
When we belong to you,
we can live on an entirely new plain
through the power of your Holy Spirit.

May we always allow your Spirit to lead us.
When we are pulled in different directions -
the compulsion of old habits
the attraction of sin,
our natural desires,
in conflict with your divine will –
please take control of us:
cut off the oxygen supply to everything
that would pull us downwards.

Lord, remind us that the battle is lifelong
and none of us can avoid it:
one of your greatest spiritual warriors
constantly felt himself pulled down
by a negative force
opposed to his good intentions.
Even the great biblical heroes
had to keep their guard up!

Thank you, Father, that
no matter what the opposition,
we are always on the winning side:
Jesus himself proclaimed the final victory
in his triumphant shout from the cross:
'It is finished!'
Hallelujah!

Ambassadors
for
Christ

Gen. 1:4; John 3:16; Luke 15:13;
1 Cor. 9:16; 2 Cor. 5:18-20

Creator and Redeemer,
I never cease to wonder
at your creative power and ingenuity:
how lovingly you conceived the universe
and brought it into being.
You made the earth
to be our perfect environment;
with breath-taking precision
you positioned the sun
at exactly the right distance
to make our world habitable;
the merest fraction of a hair's breadth
nearer or further away
and life as we know it could not exist.

Lord, I stand amazed
and over-awed by your divine workmanship!
But now I am reminded of something
even more wonderful,
more inconceivable,
more amazing:

Your Word *My Prayer*

you not only created
such an incredibly marvellous world for us,
you loved us *so much* that you gave us
your most precious gift –
your only Son.

That shows how far you were prepared to go
to bring us back from that far country
in which we were hopelessly lost –
separated from you by our sin.
That is the sacrifice you were willing to make
so that we might enjoy eternal life
and be with you for ever.

Help me to share this good news
with those I meet in my daily life.
Give me the gifts that will make me
a faithful and effective ambassador for you,
while being loving and sensitive
when representing you to others.
If I am lost for words,
guide me with your wisdom.
May I always be concerned for the whole person,
remembering to bring
his or her needs to you in prayer.

May the goodness and grace
you have showered upon me
be my constant motivation
in the responsibility and privilege
of passing on the message of your love.

Good
stewards

Matt. 25:14-15; Rom. 6:16; 1 Cor. 4:2; 12:11, 7;
1 Peter 4:10; Luke 12:48; Phil. 4:13

Gracious and generous God,
I have nothing to offer you
but the gifts you have freely given to me.
Everything I am,
everything I possess,
comes from you alone.
In calling me to be your steward
you have gifted me with the ability
to do everything that you require of me.
May I always take my responsibilities seriously,
mindful of the privilege of being entrusted
with a work to do for you, my God.

Teach me that the secret of good stewardship
lies in total obedience to you:
give me the strength to put your will above my own.
Thank you for the life and freedom you promise
to those who surrender themselves to your lordship.

Your Word *My Prayer*

Help me to recognise and appreciate the gifts of others:
may we work together in dependence on your Holy Spirit,
who perfectly distributes his gifts between us
enabling us to make our own special contribution
to the common good.

As we delight in one another's talent
may we also seek to use the gifts you give us
to share your blessing with others.

I praise you, Lord, that you have called and gifted me
to be an influence in your world;
but help me to remember that –
however great or small my ability –
the only thing you look for in my stewardship
is faithfulness in the work you give me to do.

You are my gracious Master.
You will not demand from me more than I can give
but, in all fairness, will expect full measure
from all that you have entrusted to me.
May I never disappoint you.

In confidence I trust myself to you,
relying on you alone
to fulfil all your good purposes for my life.
Thank you for Jesus, who will surely strengthen me
to do all that you ask of me.

A new

purpose

Ps. 40:5; 86:5; Jer. 2:2; Ezek. 16:60; Rom. 5:1-2;
Job 5:8-9; 2 Cor. 12:9

Dearest loving Father,
I can't get over how good you are to me!
You never reject me,
never stop loving me.
When I turn to you in my need
you are always ready to forgive me.

And this is how it's always been,
ever since the day when you found me
confused and feeling I'd lost my way in life.
You gave me your gracious promise
and I trusted it:
you will always and forever
keep your word to me.

From that moment you set me right.
You gave me peace of mind,
a new purpose in life,
and a hope I'd never known before.

Your Word *My Prayer*

Let me never take the privileges of this new life for granted.
As I trust myself to you each day,
remind me of the wonders of your grace,
and the unimaginable greatness of your power.
Help me to be receptive to all that you wish to do
in me and through me.

Numberless opportunities open up for me
because of your power and goodness.
Help me to believe
that I can reach my full potential in Jesus.

He has promised me that his grace is all I need,
his power being perfected in my weakness.
Today, I offer you my weakness
and I go out in your strength.

Grace and gratitude

Deut. 8:10-11; Luke 17:12-19; 1 Tim. 4:4-5;
Rom. 14:6; Prov. 10:22; Ps. 103:1-3

Father God,
you know how happy it makes us
when our children show appreciation
for the good life we try to give them.
We know you must feel
just the same about us.
You are so good to us:
How easy it is, though,
to take your generous gifts for granted.

But how quickly we turn to you for help
when we are in need!
Like children we run to you
with our hurts and disappointments,
problems and anxieties,
crying for you to make us better.
And when you do, we're so happy and
we breathe a sigh of relief
and get on with our lives again.

Dear Lord, please forgive us
when we so often forget to thank you.
Help us to appreciate every gift from you:
not just all the good food and drink we enjoy
on special days of celebration,
but the simple diet,

and the life-giving basic elements
that sustain us day by day.

Lord, make *me* grateful for
all the good things you give to *me*,
and bless them as I use them in your service.

May I always honour you in my eating.
Keep me from being critical of another's life-style:
let me look, rather, at my own feeding habits
that I may guard against
greed or extravagance,
and becoming indifferent
to the suffering of the hungry.
I pray that the rich nations of the world
will share more of your bounty
with those countries
where people struggle to survive
poverty, drought or famine.
But help me also to remember that
many of your children
will go to bed hungry tonight,
and give me love enough to share what I have.

Thank you, Father
for all the good things
you generously give me.
My life is enriched by your many gifts,
which I can do nothing to earn or deserve.

I am overwhelmed by such grace!
May I show my gratitude
with thanksgiving that comes
sincerely from my heart.
I praise you for your loving kindness.
May your holy name be blessed for ever.

Waiting for God

Ps. 27:14; 62:1; Isa. 40:31; 55:3; 65:24;
Rom. 8:11; Eph. 1:18-19; Rom. 8:2

Great Father,
Yes, it's me, . . .
needing to spend time quietly in your presence.
No hurry.
This is so important to me:
I need your saving power because
only you can restore me,
and make me whole.

Help me to make this quiet time a daily priority,
so that I may be strengthened and find courage
through the power of your Spirit.
May I never think that I'm too busy
to meet with you in prayer:
to wait for you . . .
quietly, expectantly . . .

Thank you for your promise
that as I wait on you
I shall be lifted out of my heaviness:
my spirit set free
to soar upwards,
reaching new heights.
Resting in your presence,
my weariness will drop away,
my strength be renewed,

and with you beside me
I shall feel ready
to take on the world!

May I continually draw on the power
of your indwelling Holy Spirit to lift me up:
that very same power
by which you raised
Jesus from the grave.

I can hardly get my mind round
the amazing spiritual power available to me.
Open my eyes to see just what it means.
Help me to understand,
to believe,
to take hold of
all that you are holding out to me.

Thank you that following you
means being under new management:
gone is the old life
dominated by rules and regulations,
guilt and penalties.
Now I live under the law
of the Spirit of Christ
which sets me free
from the downward pull
of sin and death.

My prayer takes on
a new sense of expectancy
when I believe that you hear me:
yes, that even before I start speaking,
you are at work
answering my prayer.

Eternal Life

Mark 10:15; Matt. 5:3; Rev. 3:20; John 6:37; 15:1-5;
Isa. 30:15; 46.4; Zech. 4:6; Rom. 8:37

My Father,
Just as little children
never doubt their parents' love –
never seek to analyse it,
never question it,
simply accept it –
help me to have that same child-like trust
so that I never doubt that
you will lovingly welcome me
into your kingdom.

How I thank you, Lord Jesus – Brother –
that I can actually come to you
on equal terms,
with nothing to commend me:
deserving nothing,
bringing nothing
except my desperate need
of your grace.

Others, too.
How patiently you wait for us
to open up our lives to you –
never overriding our wills
forcing your way in
taking over without our permission.

Instead, you hold everything out to us
and long for us to accept
your friendship,
your new life,
your salvation.

However long it takes us to respond
you never withdraw your invitation.
Thank you for your promise
to everyone who comes to you
that you will never reject them.

Lord, you tell me to live in you
and allow you to live in me:
you could not have explained
the secret of living a vital and fruitful life
more simply.
May your life radiate through me each day.

May I live in total dependence upon you
constantly returning and resting,
seeking forgiveness,
renewing my strength,
and opening my life to your Spirit
that I may experience your saving power.

Thank you that you have undertaken
responsibility for our lives:
you created us,
and have cared for us over the years,
through good and bad times,
and your love will continue to support us
through the frailty of old age
and to the very end of our lives.

Strength for today

Deut. 33:27; Mark 13:11; Matt. 6:34;
Isa. 30:18; 40:28-29; 2 Cor. 12:8-10; Phil. 4:13

Blessed Lord,
any day of my life
can bring unforeseen problems,
catching me completely unaware.
When troubles arise
help me to rest my full weight
on your promises which never fail:
your strong and loving arms
will surely carry me through each day
whatever it might bring.

Sometimes I feel
my back is to the wall,
as I find myself hemmed in
by destructive forces.
I feel so weak and helpless to defend myself.
Even worse, I am a poor witness to you
as I feebly argue your cause.
Whenever I feel threatened
keep me from saying
the first thing that comes into my head.
Remind me of your promise

Your Word *My Prayer*

that your Holy Spirit will prompt me
with the right words –
if only I will *listen!*

I know I can be confident that
you will take care of everything.
I can have real peace about the future.

You are the everlasting God:
the mighty Creator of the universe.
You recharge the batteries
of those whose energy is depleted.
You encourage the faint hearted
and uphold with your power
those who feel weak and defeated.
I know I can trust you to help me
when I fear my life is falling apart.

How reassured I feel
as I remember your promise
that your power is perfected in my weakness.
Thank you for boosting my confidence
when I recognise my frailty
and bring it to you.
You, who can use it
to bring glory to yourself.
When others see what you can do –
yes, even through me –
they can only praise you
for the victory you give me.
Surely, when I am weak
I am truly strong –
because I depend on you alone,
through Christ who strengthens me.

No pit so deep

Isa. 38:17; 1 John 4:9-10; Micah 7:18-19;
Ps. 30:2-3; 40:1-2; Jonah 2:7

Dear Lord and Father,
so many today feel themselves to be
trapped in a dark pit from which there's no escape:
I think of those trapped
in addiction,
in poverty or crippling debt;
those in the pit of despair,
loneliness or alienation;
those in the sorrow of a fractured relationship,
suffering rejection and heartbreak.
Perhaps the deepest pit of all is that of guilt.
Can there be anyone who hasn't been there?
Surely not, and that is why
you sent your Son into our world,
to redeem us and give us new life in him.

What love you displayed as your great rescue plan
broke into our history
in a way that was to change everything for ever.
It was not our feeble love for you,
but your undeserved love for us that made you act
to rescue us from the pit of hopeless failure.
In your great love you gave your Son
to bear our sin and set us free.

Your Word *My Prayer*

Who is a God like you?
You have every right
to be angry with us for ever,
but you choose to let your anger go,
and you delight to show mercy.
In your compassion you put our sins out of your sight,
sinking them in the depths of the ocean,
as if they were deadly radioactive waste.
What a relief this is for us!

Father God
in my own spiritual sickness and depression
I cried to you for help and you healed me.
You lifted me up from that dark pit
where I felt so alone and far from you;
you restored my life.

In the silence I waited for you –
it was all I could do.
Who else but you could help me?
And all the while
you were working from the other side.
Yes, you pulled me up out of that miserable place,
out of the mire of sin and despair
in which I was sinking;
you brought me up into the light
and made me to walk tall again
in the security of your presence.
Who is a God like you?
My God and my Rock of Salvation!

Battle
for the
mind

Jer. 9:5; Rom. 5:1-2; 7:23-24; Matt. 11:28;
Heb. 4:10; Phil. 3:9; 2 Cor. 3:18

Dear God,
I come to you today in two minds.
On the one hand I feel depressed and angry
as all around me I see the signs of a sick society:
rising crime and anti-social behaviour,
alcohol and drug abuse,
greed and exploitation,
racial disharmony –
I could go on and on . . . . .

But then, on the other hand,
I'm only too aware of my own weaknesses.
How far short I fall of your standards!
Who am I to criticise?
I know what I ought to do –
what I want to do –
and yet there seems to be within me an insidious power
pulling me down like some negative force of moral gravity.
I feel ashamed, and so helpless.

But now I call to mind the words of Jesus,
inviting me to come to him just as I am.

And so I come;
defeated, discouraged, sick of myself;
to experience again that perfect peace
which Jesus has won for me
by his victory on the cross.
Through his saving death
I am welcomed into your holy presence,
and because of your amazing grace
I can even look forward
to sharing your glory!

Father, I thank you that I can look forward
to a full and perfect rest
at the end of my earthly pilgrimage.

Right now I let go of striving to deal
with my sense of sin and failure;
of trying to put myself right with you.
You have declared me *not guilty*
because Jesus has taken all my sin and blame upon himself.

Thank you so much
that your Holy Spirit is at work in my life,
restoring your image within me.
Help me to open up more of my life
to his transforming power.
Please help me to be more like Jesus.

Daily work

Hag. 2:4; John 15:5; Phil. 4:13; Isa. 35:3-4; Judges 6:14;
Rom. 8:31; 2 Cor. 4:1; Gal. 6:9; 1 Cor. 15:57

Dear Lord,
I come to you today, asking for your help
in the ordinary daily tasks
you have set before me.
There's nothing spectacular about them.
To others who lead more adventurous lives,
much of what I do each day
would seem routine, monotonous,
and undemanding.
But the exciting thing is
that they are part of your plan for my life
and I want to be strong enough
to perform them well.

Help me to stay close to you
so that your life can flow into me
and through me,
nourishing and strengthening me
just as a vine feeds its branches
with life-giving sap.

Dear Father, you know all about my bad days:
those mornings when I wake up feeling unequal
to what the new day threatens to bring.
May I always turn to you as a first resource,

confident that you will encourage
and strengthen me,
and deliver me from my fears.
You will surely work things out for me.

Whenever I am faced with
a seemingly impossible task,
give me faith to believe
that whatever you call me to do,
you will help me to accomplish.
With you beside me
I cannot fail.

You more than outweigh
all the difficulties stacked against me.
You are all I need:
with you on my side
no human or spiritual power
can get the better of me.

So, Lord, why should I be down-hearted?
I press ahead with the work in hand –
the big tasks and the little ones:
together, we'll get the job done
as long as I remain centred in your will
and serve you with enthusiasm.
Your purpose will be fulfilled
just as long as I don't get diverted
or allow myself to be discouraged.

Fill me with a spirit of thanksgiving
as I celebrate the victory
you have promised me in Jesus, my Lord.

Comforting

strength

2 Cor. 1:3-4; Ps. 103:13-14; Isa. 66:13;
1 Peter 5:7; John 14:16-17; Rev. 21:4

Compassionate Lord, Father of Jesus,
thank you that you are always there for me.
You promise to strengthen me in weakness
and comfort me in trouble,
to support me in all my trials and difficulties.

You know each of your children so well –
you alone can care for us with such compassion.
You deal so patiently with our weakness and failure,
and continually make allowance for our human frailty.
Whatever would we do without you?

When we cry out to you,
as little children cry for their parent in the night,
you hurry to our side,
taking us in your strong arms
and comforting us with your love.

Dear Father, you know all about
my nagging doubts,
my secret fears,
the temptations that try me,
the habits that defeat me.
In this quiet moment in your presence,

Your Word *My Prayer*

I let go every concern and anxiety . . . .
every sin and failure . . . .
all my guilt and regrets . . . .
I turn them over to you,
confident that I can trust you
with every care that weighs me down.
You have revealed yourself as a God
who is full of grace and mercy.

Thank you so much that Jesus
made provision for his friends before he left them;
thank you that he did not leave us to fend for ourselves.
How good it is to have the companionship of your Holy Spirit –
to know that he lives within us,
guiding and strengthening us with his divine power.
Thank you that his comforting presence will never leave us.

Thank you that we can look forward
to that unimaginably wonderful day
when we shall be comforted as never before.
When you yourself will wipe away all tears from our eyes,
and we shall never have cause to weep again.
No more sickness and dying!
No more parting and grieving!
No more death!
Everlasting sunshine in the joy of your presence!
HALLELUJAH!

God's
willingness

Matt. 7:7-8; 7:11; 1 John 5:14-15;
James 1:5; Ps. 34:15,17

Faithful God,
like any loving, caring parent
you want your children to come to you
for anything they need.
What could be more natural?
Yet all too often we miss out
because we fear that our requests
are too trivial,
or we think you have
far more important things to concern you.

Help us to take you at your word;
to hear again the simplicity
of your invitation
to ask – that we may receive,
to seek – only to find,
to knock – and find the door open wide in welcome.

Persuade our uncertain minds
that as we align our wills
to your divine purpose
you not only hear us,

you straightway begin to act on our behalf.
We don't have to badger you,
as if you were reluctant to respond to us.
We have only to trust in your willingness
to meet us in our need.

Faced with the problems
and complexities of life,
we sometimes feel completely out of our depth.
We need your help:
give us your wisdom,
and point us in the right direction.
Thank you that we only have to ask
and you will show us the right course of action.

Thank you that you are the best of parents:
you know each one of us and our individual needs
so personally and intimately.
We are never out of your sight,
or earshot.
You hear our first cry of anxiety or trouble,
and then you take care of us,
making everything all right again!

Lord, you are *greater*

Ps. 55:22; 61:2; 63:3, 5-6; 94:19; Isa. 38:14;
1 Kings 3:7; James 1:5; Rom. 7:18; Matt. 9:2, 22

God, my Father and Friend,
when I'm weighed down with cares and anxiety,
at my wits end
and unable to cope with it all,
how I need your help!
Only you can quieten my mind
and rekindle my hope.
Only you can make me smile again.

When the pressures of life are overwhelming,
remind me that you are greater
than any problem that besets me.
You have the power to
overcome every difficulty,
remove every obstacle,
heal every hurt.
You are the solid bedrock of my life;
draw me to yourself and keep me safe.

When negative thoughts
invade my mind,
giving me nightmares
and disturbing my peace,
help me to remember your promise,
and to cry to you for help.

You invite me to unload
all my burdens of care and anxiety upon you.

Your Word *My Prayer*

What a relief to know
you will lift me up
and hold me safe!

Lord, sometimes things happen
that confuse and disturb me.
When I hear or read about
some of the terrible things
that go in your world,
it nearly blows my mind.
I feel like a helpless child,
completely out of my depth.
I don't know anything any more.
I have no words.

But you are the glorious, all-wise God.
You are always ready to give me
the wisdom I lack:
I have only to ask.

And now I come to you, O Lord.
I cast my restlessness upon you
even as I struggle with guilt and failure.
However hard I try
I still keep falling down.

I am so grateful
for your personal assurance
that you will forgive me
and restore me to wholeness of life.

I praise you, dear Father
for your loving kindness:
for giving me all that my heart could desire
so that I overflow with joy.
May your steadfast love
be the theme of my prayer
throughout this day
and into the silent hours of the night.

Humble
service

Acts 20:19; Matt. 20:26-28; Gal. 6:3;
Rom. 12:3; Luke 17:10; 2 Cor. 1:12; 4:7; 12:9

Dearest Father,
teach me the secret of serving you
with a humble mind.

You know how much I enjoy
taking centre stage –
being in charge of others
who will look up to me
and be impressed with my every little achievement.
How far short I fall
of the example Jesus gave us:
showing by word and action
that he had come to fulfil a servant's role,
even to the point of sacrificing his life
so that we could be set free.

When I have inflated ideas about my gifts,
and get carried away in self-delusion,
bring me down to earth.
Help me to get real about myself.
I'm no use to you living in a fantasy world.

I'd like to have a true estimate
of the gifts you have given me,
so that I appreciate them and
use them humbly in your service,

giving all the credit to you.
Everything of value in my life
is due to your grace –
yes, even my faith in you.

May the ordinary business
of my everyday life
be enhanced by the joy
of knowing that I am serving you.
Help me to keep in mind
that each day is your gift to me,
which I can offer back to you.

I pray for your grace;
may it permeate everything I do and say,
so that I will be open and sincere
in all my dealings with others.

Help me to accept
that my flawed human nature
will bring me problems and failure.
For all that, I need not be discouraged
because my very weakness
is an opportunity for more of your grace
to shine through!

And that's the bottom line:
your grace is all I need
for your power is perfected in my weakness.
Thank you, Father.

God's
light
in
us

John 8:12; Luke 11:34; 1 Cor. 2:10, 14;
Ps. 119:18; 2 Cor. 3:18; 4:6; Eph. 1:17-18

My Father in Heaven,
thank you for the revelation
that Jesus is the light of the world,
and if I trust in him
I need never be afraid of the dark again.
Just as when the sun breaks through
the clouds of a cheerless day,
lifting my spirits
and making me glad to be alive,
so his light streams
into every part of my being,
bringing healing, spiritual growth
and guidance for the way ahead.

I love to welcome his light –
to let it shine into every part of my life.
It helps keep my eyes focused on you,
as I endeavour to stay single-minded
in my desire to please you.

You have made this possible
through the gift of your Holy Spirit,
who lives and shines within all who follow Jesus.
How foolish –
how utterly beyond understanding –
this is to those who will not allow his Spirit
to open their eyes to your truth.

Your Word *My Prayer*

As I read and study the Bible,
give me a fresh insight into your word:
open my spiritual eyes,
that I may not miss out
on the wonderful treasures
sparkling within its pages.

Filled with your Spirit,
I am being transformed
into the image of your Son:
I am even beginning to reflect
a little of his beauty and brightness!
Oh yes, I know it's going to take for ever,
but your Spirit is always working within me
to complete the transformation.

Just as you first commanded
the light to shine in the darkness,
so you continue to light up my life
with the knowledge of your glory
revealed to humankind
in the beauty of Jesus, your Son.

I praise you, Almighty Father,
Tender God of power and glory,
for all the wonderful things
you are showing to your people.
Give us a spirit of wisdom and understanding
that we may come to know you better
in our Lord Jesus Christ.
Open our eyes to the hope
to which you have called us –
supremely, the promise
of sharing together in our rich inheritance:
all your goodness, grace and glory
for ever and for ever!

in me

Isa. 5:4; 40:30-31; Ps. 46:10; John 14:6; 15:4;
2 Tim. 2:11; Eph. 2:14; Rev. 21:5

Faithful God,
when I look at the Lord Jesus,
realising who he is
and all he has suffered for me,
I stand amazed
and overwhelmed by such love.
I hear you speaking to me, asking me:
What more could I have done?

I simply want to rest quietly in your presence,
knowing in the depth of my spirit
that you are God,
almighty, righteous, holy Lord,
my heavenly Father.
In the stillness
I wait patiently for you,
trusting in your promise
that those who wait on you
will be renewed in strength:
they will be lifted up
as though on eagles' wings,
supported by the rising thermals
of your Holy Spirit.
They will run and not be exhausted,
will walk and not faint.

Your Word *My Prayer*

You tell me that the simple yet profound secret
of true spiritual life
is to abide in Jesus
and allow him to live in me.
Help me to live this truth –
to practise it daily.

Help me to realise that
the new life I enjoy in Christ
was opened up to me when he died on the cross.
Now, as I hand back my life to him,
seeking to subdue my own selfish desires,
he raises me up
into his resurrection life.
That is where I am right now.

May I keep his word in my heart:
I am the way, the truth, the life.
May I know that he is my way through life
because he walks with me.
That he is the truth about life
because he has clearly shown me what you are like.
That he *is* the life
because only in him can I live life to the full –
daily enjoying the abundant life he promises.

As I live in him and he lives in me,
may your perfect peace
fill my life to overflowing.

As I quietly, trustfully,
dwell in him and he in me,
may I know that you are at work within me,
transforming me
and making new every part of me,
even to the depths of my being.

 **than
conquerors**

Ps. 60:4; Exod. 17:15; Isa. 59:19; Ps. 20:5; Luke 23:33;
Jer. 51:10; Rom. 8:37; 1 Cor. 15:57; Eph. 6:10;
Hag. 2:4; John 4:35; Heb. 10:37

Almighty God,
your word tells us that
when you led your people forward,
you encouraged them
by displaying a victorious banner.

I want to thank you today
that when we are facing difficulty or danger
you put new heart into us as we remember
that *you yourself* are that victory standard!

Help us to be confident that,
just like a river in full flood,
your power can sweep away every obstacle.

As we proudly nail our colours to your mast,
keep us rejoicing in your saving power.

Help us to be truly grateful for all the benefits
Jesus has won for us:

Your Word *My Prayer*

our claim to righteousness is founded entirely
upon his finished work at Calvary.
May this always be our testimony
as we seek to share our faith with others.

Help us to know that in every circumstance of life
we are more than conquerors through your love.

Thank you that Jesus was victorious in his death.
May we never doubt that he is able
to help us to be victorious too.

There is no need for us to give in to the temptation
to rely on our own human resources.
Keep us trusting in the strength
which he alone can give us.

Help us to put your will before our own
and give us the courage
to work at the tasks you set us.

Give us a spirit of expectancy and enthusiasm
for all that you have planned for us.
And may we live each day
mindful that your glorious appearing
draws ever closer.
AMEN

The final battle

1 Cor. 13:12; Heb. 2:8; 2 Peter 1:19; Ps. 119:105;
Jude 17-18; 1 Tim. 4:1; 1 John 2:18;
Rom. 13:12; Eph. 6:13-16

Omnipotent, gracious Father,
the more I learn about you,
the more conscious I am of how little I know.
I come to you
with a mind full of questions:
there is so much I would like to ask you
face to face.

You have given all power and authority
to the Lord Jesus,
and as I wait for his promised return
give me patience to accept
that not everything is yet subject to him.
Help me to live with this tension.

During this time of waiting,
you have revealed to me
everything I need to know for now.
One day the full radiance of the light of your truth
will illuminate my mind.

Meantime, keep me trusting
that the light of your word
will clearly mark out the way ahead for me.

Your Word *My Prayer*

Father, you have told us that we must expect
to meet with cynical opposition
from the enemies of your truth:
those who would ridicule your people
and live only to indulge their sinful
and selfish pleasure.

Even more so is the threat
from those evil spiritual powers at work all around us,
seeking to destroy our faith in you.

Help us to be encouraged
as we read in your word
that all this enemy activity signals
the fast-approaching return of the Lord Jesus.

And so, heavenly Father,
we rejoice
that the night of perplexity,
of rampant evil,
of unrelieved suffering,
is drawing to a close.
The day of your glorious new life
will soon be breaking.
Help us to clear out of our lives
everything tainted with the works of darkness.

Help us to clothe ourselves
with your protecting armour of light:
faith, righteousness, truth and peace.
Make us determined to fight for your cause
and to seize every opportunity to share with others
the good news of your saving grace.

Praise
song

Ps. 86:12; 92:1-2; 150:6; Rom. 12:1;
Heb. 13:12, 15; Rev. 5:12

My Lord and my God,
everything within me wants to thank you
for all you mean to me.
You never stop loving me.
Your grace and your goodness
never fail to embrace me.
I will honour your Name
every day that you give me life.
You deserve to receive my whole-hearted praise.

Every morning I feel like singing to you,
in praise of all your steadfast love for me:
each night I go to bed telling myself how blessed I am.
I fall asleep in the comforting assurance
that you will never leave me,
never let me down.
Father God, help me to remember
that the praise I offer you with my lips
must find its final expression
in the offering of my life
as a daily sacrifice of service.
I find a spirit of worship in the work you entrust to me,
and I pray that the manner of my living
will always be acceptable to you,
never causing you to be ashamed of me.

Your Word *My Prayer*

How can I ever forget
that Jesus gave his all for me –
suffering shame and rejection,
laying down his life
as a perfect sacrifice for my sin.
Through him, I offer you now
my praise and thanksgiving:
may my worship be warmed
by the memory of all he has done for me.
May your Name be honoured
in my every word and deed.

You are worthy, my God,
to receive the highest praise that your people can offer:
Let everything in creation resound with your praise!
May every flower be seen,
as a revelation of your creative skill,
every birdsong an anthem to rejoice your Creator heart.
Let every leaf bud witness
to your resurrection power,
every spring-time
herald your promise of everlasting life.
May every sunrise
make us conscious of your controlling hand –
every star-lit night
your infinite greatness.
Let all creation praise you, O Lord!

And may the praises of your people
rise to heaven itself,
where Jesus our Lord is enthroned:
the Lamb of God, given for the world.
We join our voices with the angelic choir:
You are worthy of honour and glory and praise
for ever and ever
Amen!

Deepening

faith

Gal. 4:4-7; Rom. 4:20-21; 14:13; 15:1; Mark 4:40;
Matt. 9:28-29; Luke 17:5; Jude 20; 1 Peter 5:10

Thank you, heavenly Father,
for giving me faith to believe and trust in Jesus.
In your perfect plan
you sent him into our world to set us free.
Now I don't have to be weighed down with guilt
because of continual failure
to live up to your standards.
Because you have adopted me as your own child
I know I am accepted by you
just as I am.

Dear Father, living within your family
is a totally new and satisfying experience.
Through your Holy Spirit
I now have faith to live my life
in a close, intimate relationship with you.
Even more, I can expect to receive from you
the good things which all loving parents
delight to share with their children.

Give me a faith that will withstand
every testing circumstance;
Give me a faith that will grow stronger
with each difficulty I have to face,
so that I may become strong and mature in my spiritual life.

Your Word *My Prayer*

When my faith is weak
I get discouraged and give myself a bad time.
But then I remember:
even those great apostles disappointed Jesus:
'Where is your faith;
Why did you doubt me?'
How well he understood them.
Just so, I believe, he knows me.

Give me the faith, dear Father,
to believe that Jesus still works miracles:
that today he is still willing and able
to heal me physically and spiritually
and so make me whole.

Lord, those first disciples of Jesus
were mindful of their need of faith.
Just as they came to you with that need,
so I ask you to satisfy my longing
for a faith that will grow ever stronger.

Day by day, as I seek you in prayer,
help me to draw on all the resources
of your Holy Spirit.

Thank you, Father,
that every good thing
is given to me freely by your grace,
and that, ever before me, is the promise
of one day sharing your glory.

Your Word *My Prayer*

Help me to accept
that suffering may be part of the process
by which you are refining me,
as you guide me towards
what you want me to be.

Forgive me when I am impatient with others:
help me to accept the weaknesses
of those who are still young in the faith,
and to encourage rather than criticise them.

Keep me from being judgemental,
or causing another to stumble.
I would hate to unsteady anyone's faith
when I want so much to be strong in my own.